The Effects of Grace

A Collection of Christian Poetry

The Effects of Grace © 2015 by TL Publishing Group

Original cover art ©

Cover art design by © Alice Shantel Saunders

Edited by Alice Saunders and

Published by TL Publishing Group

ISSN- 10: 978-0692597200
ISBN-13: 0692597204

TL Publishing Group
www.torridliterature.com

Dedication

To His Children, both lost and found.

Table of Contents

And God is able to make all grace [every favor and earthly blessing] come in abundance to you, so that you may always [under all circumstances, regardless of the need] have complete sufficiency in everything [being completely self-sufficient in Him], and have an abundance for every good work and act of charity.

2 Corinthians 9:8 (AMP)

The Greatest Love Affair
Author: Audrey Burke Moore

Even in marriage, I can't forget him...he is my past, my present and all in between and I would be lost if he did not love me. For he is the only one that can mend my scars with bandages torn from the hem of his garment and he is the only one that can heal my wounds given to me by life simply within his one suture, he is my life and no one comes before him....he is my now, and all I need in my future.....

He is the breath that I breathe...he is fulfilling. I have never felt love that enraptures the whole body including the soul. His attention lies with every piece of my being, and I am perfect in his eyes. When all else fails, he stands strong for me, he lets me fight the battles that arise in life, but when I let go, he fights for my name.......I give him honor for he is constant.....he always remains

He never plants the seed of doubt in my mind because all things are possible through him. If ever I begin to feel as if I am suffocating he sends a bouquet of fresh air to my door. Once when I was scared and thought I was in in harm, I looked for him and noticed he had me safe within his arms.

I love to wake up in the morning and just shout out is name...........El Roi for he sees me, Elohim because his power is amazing, El Shaddai because he moves mountains for me, Jehovah for he never changes, Rohi because I am but a lamb, Rapha because he heals me, Adonai because he is great.

For all the names I can call him, he gives me blessings I can't afford, so if you ask me to name who is my love affair with, it's simple.....he is My Life, My God, My Lord.

The Priestly Figure

By Cardiwel Ebuse

for the memory of Gerard Manley Hopkins

The priestly figure stands before my eyes.
His garb's triangular in many parts,
adorned with number one, to emphasize
his godliness, which is way off the charts.
O, God, one wants to be his follower
in order just to reach such holiness,
from head to toe, from thigh to collar-bone,
to be God's [hockey] soccer-playing goalee—yes!
And though this priestly man is wrinkled (His
skin ripples down his body's length in folds.)
there's something thrilling in all that he is,
inspiring in the posture that he holds.
He makes me want t' embrace his hard [earned/won] doctrine,
and strive to be as trim—to block out sin,
                              a hawk in wind.

Fighting Loopholes
By Jordan Legg

The thieves my lust manufactured
appear so innocent and friendly,
as they materialize in my mind
and manifest on the monitor.
But behind their conjured smiles
lies the malice of fraudulence.
They've stolen from me, my wife, my God.
They massage my ego,
and claim that they're loopholes
instead of infractions.
If I loved You, I wouldn't look for loopholes.
Fighting them off does no good,
it only increases the flattery that pixilated Sirens sing.
Help!
Get them away from me, because I can't do it by myself.
I know You're sweeter, deeper, realer than they will ever be.
Let me fall into You.
Your blood corrodes the grime
that holds the empty-handed prodigal,
and frees him to run into Your grace.

Not Me

By Peter Venable

Credo ergo sum- "I believe, therefore I am"
Rests deeper than Descartes's dictum "I think"—
More subtle than a Myers-Briggs exam
Or analysis from a patronizing shrink.

This thing called "Self"—a cryptogram, is worded code,
Stretching between what I am and am not.
The griefs of life in the mirror erode
And in between, my soul entreats "Out, out damned spot."

I believe I am not up to the bar, the grade
Despite my sweat, my tears, my lottery dream
Or when I held to truth or when I strayed.
It is in You I find my cipher Self redeemed.

Storm

By Jason Kirk Bartley

The trial rages on,
The storm clouds up ahead,
I toss and I turn, cannot get to bed.
My sea is swelling the tide is crashing,
Waves are falling, but my name He's calling.
Jesus reaches down as I sink beneath the waves,
My faith and trust completely in that the Father completely saves.
So though my world is crumbling,
Seems like every day I take a tumbling in the lessons Of life.
But my foundation sure, my eyes are fixed, heart is pure,
Jesus will not fail, He is my sail, my strength, my rock, my deliverer
through the storm.

Jesus Stepped In
By Jason Kirk Bartley

He thought he had forever,
Forever became not enough.
Living day to day,
Life was rough.
It came down upon him like a ton of sand
Crushing his hopes and dashing his plans.
Now here he sits with a shotgun to kill.
The shotgun was ever pulled out of its case,
It came out on special occasions when troubles
he did not want to face.
This time he'd been drinking, he was a scared little man.
Pierced at the soul,
Had taken all he could stand.
As he began to pull the trigger,
Something wanted to talk it over.
He felt such a calm feeling come over him then,
This was the perfect moment when Jesus stepped in.
"My Child, My child, what seems to be the pain. I died for you.
Cast it upon me. Take it to your Lord, He will show you mercy."
That night Jesus began to reign as he asked Jesus in.
No more would he be plagued by the guilt of sin.
He had been adopted, had been taken in.
Thank God for mercy,
Jesus stepped in.

Saved By Grace
By Jason Kirk Bartley

I'm a work in progress.
Far from complete.
Jesus picked me up.
I was dead on my feet.
Dancing with the Devil
In a world of sin.
Everything changed when
Jesus stepped in.
I could not have done it,
Not on my own.
God had to cleanse me turn me around.
Nothing I've done or earned,
But God's gift to me for turning
everything over to Him.
Eternally.

His Smile
By: Michelle Bayha

By God's grace
He walked me to my car,
Reminding me to turn on the headlights,
Waving to me happily,
Murmuring "Goodbye sweetheart."

By God's grace
He told the funniest stories,
Embellishing details to our delight,
In the most enthusiastic tone,
As we laughed until we cried.

By God's grace
He released his pain to God
Embracing the love we gave him,
Remembering us all,
Until his last breath.

By God's grace
He watches over us:
His wife, children, and grandchildren
Breathing a sigh of relief
Because he is happy in heaven

By God's grace,
His family looks to the higher being,
For strength as they struggle to carry on.
Burdened by their loss of him,
They cherish his amazing smile.

He Is Able
By Dionne Evans

He is the one who created,
Who put the stars into space,
He is the one who spoke,
And it came to pass,
Jesus, the son who died and rose again,
With all power in His hand,
He is able to bring joy,
When you are sad,
He is able to bring you peace,
In the midst of the storm,
He is able to bring understanding,
When there is confusion,
He alone is capable,
Ask me how I know,
I, have tried Him many times over,
And He has never failed me yet,
This I know, He is able.

With Each Step
By Dionne Evans

As I step into uncharted waters,
I look to the One who holds the future,
I look back over my life and have seen how He has kept me,
Even when I have not always done what was right,
But I've come to realize with each step; He loves me,
For the shining light of Jesus is a lamp unto my feet,
That draws me into healing and deliverance,
For with each step I take; I can stand bold,
In Him-Jesus, who is my friend,
With each step I'm going to praise His awesome and majestic name,
For you see, besides Him, there is none other.

Waiting
By Dionne Evans

Waiting on that which you are hoping for,
Seems to be the hardest when you cannot see,
At every turn you'll think this is the open door,
To manifest itself for you to be free,
Free, from the weariness of endurance,
That comes from the toils of the night,
Yet you tell yourself "press on",
Because the end must be in sight,
Once you have arrived, you will surely say,
The waiting was worth it, all the way,
I know for certain, yes it was,
So rejoice my soul rejoice,
The wait pays off, it does.

Sailing the Sea of Life
By John Kaniecki

An endless ocean
A boundless sea
We have set sail
For eternity
The winds are fierce
The waves are high
I can never fail
If I simply try
I am not the captain
Just a simple deck hand
On this ship on the ocean
Bound for the Promised Land
The one in charge
On him we depend
He is the Lord
Our eternal friend
In Him we trust
And feel secure
That he can guides us
To heaven's shore

The Annunciation

By Philip C. Kolin

a courtier visits
from the highest heavens
salvation begins

God's scroll of light
serenading a virgin awed
in innocence, a spotless womb

lilies flaring from a cedar staff
a voice confirming creation's delight
be it done unto me

the brilliance of a shadow
be it done unto me
eternity fills emptiness

Christ clothed in flesh,
in time, in thorns, in a shroud
the heir to David's throne

to be crowned on Golgotha
heaven's handmaiden holds
a baby leaping in hosannas

from the womb
the Incarnation
why God made the world

A David

By Charis Froelich

We dreamt of a David,
With a sword in his hand and beauty in his eyes.
Who would burst through these sorrows
And give us our peace.
When we beheld the face
Of this sallow, bludgeoned serf
As he hung there in the dark
We despaired.

We thought we knew him
And we thought we knew his battle
Until we looked into his murderers' eyes
And saw our own eyes staring back

Then we knew who he'd saved us from.

Autumn

By Christina Mengis

Mother and child, sun and rain,
you make us love your holy name.
Green, red, yellow, and brown,
Death is falling to the ground.
Leaves on trees, holding on for dear life
all will fall and die in flight.
Some will hit the concrete,
and others will float to a nearby car,
it doesn't really matter because
the cycle of life and death is not far.
The birds fly south,
while the ants scurry for winter food.
All the while the leaves keep falling till their lives are renewed.
You were gone for three days, and then you came back.
My faith and love for you is something I don't lack.

Supplication
By Richard Hartwell

Preferring the groined cathedrals of medieval Europe
over the dismal creations of modern architecture,
pessimisms of all horizontal lines and earthly bound;

Preferring the vaulted arches of transepts and nave,
encouraging the eyes ever up, soaring to the One,
over bingo hall, community center, reception room;

Preferring prayers impregnated with incense, then
embryoed in wood and gestating life with grace,
over the declamations of concrete and clear glass;

       Alone or in packed pews, a presence pervades
       ancient houses of worship with a softer touch,
       a gentler hand, and the flesh tingles as angels
       flit among dust motes above carrying sin away.

We Were Strangers

By Lisbon Tawanda Chigwenjere

We were in the world, but not of the world,
We were born not of blood, but of the Word,
We did not come from an earthly location,
We were of a heavenly nation,
On earth we were just but strangers,
Yet we left as world changers,
Nothing about us deserved pity,
Our roots were of a heavenly city,
Through Christ we reigned as kings,
We mounted high with eagles' wings,
We were strangers,
Yet we left the earth as world changers

Through the power of God's wisdom,
We translated many into God's kingdom,
Together with saints like Liberty Saunders,
We did mighty miracles, signs and wonders,
We were soldiers, sent in pairs,
Not to be entangled in civilian affairs,
We were strangers,
Yet we left the earth as world changers

We were given our own pastors and teachers,
Reverend Chris Oyakhilome and others,
For the perfecting of the saints they were given,
To teach us the mysteries of the kingdom of heaven,
Till we were no more children, tossed to and fro,
Till we kept the devil under our feet, on the floor,
We were strangers,
Yet we left the earth as world changers

Count it All Joy
By Lisbon Tawanda Chigwenjere

"My brethren, count it all joy when you fall into divers temptations." (James 1:2)

When you fall into divers tests, little boy,
I want you to remember these words, "count it all joy"
I want you to rejoice,
I want you to sing a song in the loudest voice,
You will never be defeated little boy,
That's why I say, "Count it all joy"

Little boy, you play by a different set of rules,
That's why you will never ever lose,
When you pass through the rivers, they shall not overflow you,
Even the fire shall not burn you,
Whenever you fall into divers tests, little boy,
I want you to remember these words, "count it all joy"
I want you to rejoice,
I want you to sing a song in the loudest voice,
You will never be defeated little boy,
That's why I say, "Count it all joy"

What is that in Thine Hand?
By Lisbon Tawanda Chigwenjere

Wordsmith, what is that in thine hand?
Write about the effects of grace in the holy land,
Is not that ink and paper?
Write on behalf of thy maker,
Write as the Holy Ghost inspires,
Write before your time expires,
Your works will still be read in that day,
When all else has passed away

Wings of Doves
By Krista S. Mallo

Innocent and dreaming—
Spending forever together;
Purity of one mind, one body, one spirit,
Instagram memories—
a picture-perfect summer wedding day—
Our child's first breath—
This life—
This. IS. Life.
Butter-cream coated cake tiers, encircled by roses, embraced in passion;
Like something new, something borrowed;
Silent shadows as wings of doves.
There will be no end—
Together forever and ever, Amen.
Angels shield their eyes, blinded by glory and brightness and brilliance and
this—
This. IS. Life.
We love until there is no more love to give; stand for truth, but failing—
We fall on our knees,
lift hands;
And you— me— I— us— together— we—
Chase the eternal Prince of Peace.

The Fourth Masterpiece
By Courtney Liddell

Genesis 1:14-19

Sky was poached,
Clouds whipped.
Frothy with a hint of cinnamon.

Sun was molded in an instant —
Cut precise, round like chocolate truffle;
Roasted until golden.

Night blended smooth into the Sky
Obscured beyond recognition
To return as Night finished baking

Moon was prepared,
Sautéed, seasoned within the Chef's feast
Cooked briefly to perfection.

Stars were added to savor the Moon
Each rare in shape, altogether
succulent and tender.

The Chef had completed another masterpiece
Cooked flawlessly as the three before.
The fifth course scheduled next,
Along with the sixth.
Completing His divine banquet.

Your Love Is a Flowing River...

By Gonzalinho da Costa

Your love is a flowing river leading me toward isolated caverns of tranquility,
Restful as the liquid colloquy curling round and round reflective stones sitting
       in a mountain brook
Nestled high along the hem of a darkening leather tundra.
Fold me into your heart like linen
In cabinets freshly perfumed with cotton,
Bind me fast to yourself as a sash in celebration,
Cradle me in your hand where I will dwell in the cup,
Unwinding knots at the end of a day burnished by fire.

Atop a High Mountain
By Gonzalinho da Costa

I have seen a mountain. It all happened very quickly. No body could bear it were the soul there for an hour.——Mechthild of Magdeburg, The Flowing Light of the Godhead

Atop a high mountain
I beheld a river
Not of this earth
But of the sky,

Pure, blue,
Cloudless.
Bending down
To fill a glass bottle,

I saw bubbles
Rising, escaping
The opening
At the bottle top.

I lifted the bottle
To the sun,
Empty.
I tried a second,

Third time,
No water entered.
Glancing at my hand,
Dripping,

Fresh, youthful,
Smooth,
I heard a voice say,
"This water is for healing.

All who drink it
Are refreshed.
All who bathe in it

Are made well.

No one can carry this water
Down the mountain.
All must climb the mountain
To receive this water."

When the vision vanished,
I felt a delicate thirst,
Fine as dust
Yet all-consuming.

A Wind Begins
By James Ross Kelly

Three miles up a dusty forest road then a right on a less
Traveled jeep trail and into eighty acres of BLM Land
Oregon— checkerboard of Federal & private land &
Federal is fenced by the lack of Forest

On the well logged other side of the private boundary
A still smell of wild lilac, black oak & madrone
Fill an under-story & Douglas fir w/wild turkey scratch
& around the corner the road bed
Ground rolling with the duff & shows a hundred years of carpet
Through the stand of fir that shortly gives way — Sugar Pine.

Jeep trail is dusty and covered in pine needles
Uniform sugar pine comprise immense trees of five feet on the butt
Trees stretching up & the huge sugar pine cones wave w/a breeze
Madrones grow out of rings and upward as big as the large black oaks
Three hundred or more years ago an intense forest fire
Changed something
That looked pretty much like this &
As I saw an even age of the pine stand

& now the Madrones sprouted back 300 years of the
Green turning red & peeling red barked to be
Green & red vestures sprouting round the edges
of the three hundred year ago large madrone
Making this plant near a half millennia with slick leaf winding
Upward arms & as tall as they are still under
Sugar pine as gothic as church spires &
Incense of flowing pitch smelling up & down each sugar pine tree

& church the day before this walk was good,
& as I walked & meditated
A wind begins, to move these trees &
I began to sing, Hallelujah, Hallelujah, Halle…
& Living Water begins to flow oddly enough out from my
Own solar plexus and some connection & dream is now undone
As I can place my hand into this spiritual fluid &

My own heart & His & a profusion of myself is no longer apparent,
& somehow manage to keep walking,
Through the stand of sugar pine, slowly
Mind you, step by step, and the velocity seems now, like a fire hose
Now the tall trees I stand under seem to be part of
Fabric, & living water continues, & I cannot speak &

I stop walking to stand
In front of a broken topped sugar pine that dwarfs the others
With lightening scars & these other trees are its progeny
After that long ago fire & I am undone still after sixteen years
& a stream of living water has abated & abounds & still abides
& though the big ancient sugar pine has fallen, since then
I've never had a doubt since that day.

Looking for the Lightning Bolt Judgment

By Blake Kilgore

Sometimes like an idiot I melt down into lunacy refined seventy-seven times
seven times.
I wish someone would please throw me a line.
But keep watch on me, 'cause though I'm not planning on it now —
Sometimes I get bewildered mid-rescue and try to choke myself out and
drown.

How can my brain spin faster than lead unleashed down rifling at three-
thousand feet per second?
That's too many thoughts per second and too many passing trifles linking arms
with real sorrow and real pain, real disappointments and real shame.

All balance wavers while I struggle to maintain solidarity or some sense of
clarity.
Sometimes it seems it's the tragic, irony fate of me to self-destruct, like
kamikaze.
I bang, bang, bang, bang, bang, bang, bang my head angrily, desperately, but
humbly.
I long to knock loose the demon-inspired contorted thoughts of You.

You are not deceitful; You have not forgotten.
Break through, please break through!

Confusion is whirling, my head is swirling and the voices are coming too fast,
arguments like crabgrass in my consciousness.
They grow up and take over, choking spiritfruitfulness so that hope dries and I
Become first of all grenchy, then flinchy, too sensitive - don't touch me!
And I won't touch You;
yet I long for touch, raging like a fool at its self-willed absence.

The double-tongue is caught red-handed.

Claiming, then blaming...profaning.

Sometimes I start looking for the lightning bolt judgment 'cause I know I
      done pushed too far.
But instead of gripping merciless power, your palms are marked with scars.
Your eyes are stained with tears that soothingly slide forgiveness down
      sorrowful cheeks and over smiling and tender lips that long to kiss
      my downtrodden brow,
imparting healing and life and peace for the now,
hope for the future,
    and
        forgetfulness of the past.

Angels Beat Thy Wings
By Fern G. Z. Carr

Angels beat thy wings; descend to earth
  With the power of legions
Of armour-plated warriors forging into battle;
  Triumphant trumpet flourishes shall herald thy coming —
Majestic harbingers of power, glory and grace.

Descend

Descend

Descend

Enlighten us with thy radiance —
  Animate our souls with thy splendor;
Illuminate this sojourn — our earthly passage,
  Imbue us with clarity of vision.
Angels beat thy wings; descend to earth.

Seek the Lord Daily
By Janice Canerdy

For frequent failure to achieve,
I held myself in low regard.
At times unable to believe
I could succeed, I made life hard.

Ignoring any good in me,
I zeroed in on each mistake.
My weaknesses were clear to see.
I seldom gave myself a break.

When thoughts were dark and nerves were frayed,
my mind became a lonely fort.
I pondered why I hadn't prayed
or turned to loved ones for support.

Now looking back, I realize
my faith in everyone was weak.
I feared no one could empathize
with one whose life had grown so bleak.

In desperation I cried out,
"Dear God, how could I sink this low?
How could I wallow in such doubt?
Why have I traded joy for woe?"

I know that as I seek God's will,
my healing won't come overnight.
I am a work in progress still.
Most days are good; not all are bright.

****
Each time we're overwhelmed and weak,
His grace and mercy we must seek.
Through difficulties of life's race,
the Lord will never hide His face.

La Cena di Leonardo: a Rondeau
By LindaAnn Loschiavo

To make a difference, keep strong types alive,
Da Vinci works in oils, imaginative,
This art not all he's after but re-birth,
His acts revising language known on earth.
In random places, order grows, down-sized.

Unbreathing men, thirteen, take shape contrived
Around a central red-clad operative,
Light softening at so much joy, unearthed

> To make a difference.

All's calm before a final action rives,
Disorderly and damaging. Paints drive
Eyes to details of things above, new birth
Forms intimate. This supper hints at worth
Awaiting earth, ideals of love revived

> To make a difference.

The Lament of Trophies

By Kathy Buckert

Conscience sears my trophies of memory
Each one standing on a shelf of regret
The soot of shame clings to my infamy

Footsteps of grief led to my mourning war
Consequences removed from my reprisal
Acting on urges I sought my cup of revenge

I plundered their will, the core of their being
Placating the gravity of my hatred
Seizing by passion the force of my anger

The depths of my lies are my spoils of war
Silenced shame a lamenting remembrance
Of bands of disgrace I carry in my soul

But I lay my trophies down at the foot of the cross
They are no longer mine but His.
My chains of regret and shame are broken.

I am free

Falling Into Trust

By Helen Clark

I remember in the earlier days
Of my conversion, that I used to see
Your face in others' acts of love and grace
As I consistently sought only thee

Then grief and discord shattered like a bomb
And hollow, without compass or a road,
I found no balm from platitudes and psalms
As proof for non-belief I keenly sowed

'Til on my knees with nowhere left to turn
My naked heart called out to you again,
Though suffering and broken, frantic, burned,
You loved my doubts away, my dearest Friend

O Holy Spirit, dark confusion's cure
We learn to love because You love us first,
'Til doubts erased, in your hands so secure,
To be your face for someone else we thirst.

Reorienting Light, You set us free,
Transformative, alchemic Mystery.

About the Authors:

(in alphabetical order by last name)

Jason Kirk Bartley is a Christian writer from Chillicothe, Ohio. He is 39 years of age. Bartley evangelizes and reads poetry for his church. His work has appeared in online magazines, websites, and he also wrote for *www.Worthfinding.com*. Bartley loves to communicate what the Lord has given him.

Michelle Bayha resides in New Jersey. Currently, she is in her senior year of college and will graduate Montclair State University in May 2016. She had a remarkable four years there. Each experience affects her as a person and influences her poetry in a positive way. Topics that she writes about include: friendships, relationships, mental disorders, soldiers and war, individuals overcoming prejudice/stereotypes, and perseverance to overcome one's struggles. Her poems have appeared in: *What If?* (Canada), *Congruent Spaces* (online), *UK Poetry Library* (online), *Torrid Literature Journal* (US), and *Forward Poetry: The World at War: Poems from the Battlefield* (UK). "His Smile" was written in memory of her grandfather who passed away in 2014. He was not just a grandfather to her but also a dear friend that she confided in. Taken away too soon from her life, her grandfather will be missed everyday. He will always hold a special place in her heart.

Kathy Buckert holds a Master's Degree in Education from St. Michael's College in Vermont. She also holds an M.F.A in Creative Writing from Goddard College's low-residency program in Plainfield, Vermont. Her work has appeared in Stories: *The Magazine*, *Riverlit*, *The Blue Hour*, *Black Mirror Magazine*, *Electric Rather*, *Silver Birch Press*, and other publications. She is an adjunct assistant professor at Monroe Community College in Rochester, New York.

Janice Canerdy is a retired high-school English teacher from Potts Camp, Mississippi. Canerdy has been writing poetry since childhood and especially enjoys rhymed, metered poetry. She also writes flash fiction and short stories. Her poems have appeared in several publications, including *Cyclamens and Swords*, *The Artistic Muse*, *The Road Not Taken*, *The Lyric*, *Quill Books*, *Bitterroot*, *Victorian Violet*, *Westward Quarterly*, *Miracles and Ordinary Blessings* (a Whispering Angel anthology), the contest-edition anthologies of the Mississippi Poetry Society and the National Federation of State Poetry Societies, and *LIVE* (pending) a Gospel Publishing House publication.

Fern G. Z. Carr is a director of Project Literacy, lawyer, teacher and past president of the Society for the Prevention of Cruelty to Animals. She is a member of and former Poet-in-Residence for the League of Canadian Poets. Carr composes and translates poetry in five languages while currently learning Mandarin Chinese. A 2013 Pushcart Prize nominee, she has been published extensively world-wide from Finland to the Seychelles. In addition to multiple prizes and awards, honours include being cited as a contributor to the Prakalpana Literary Movement in India; her poetry having been taught at West Virginia University and set to music by a Juno-nominated musician; an online feature in *The Globe and Mail*, Canada's national newspaper; and her poem, "I Am", chosen by the Parliamentary Poet Laureate as Poem of the Month for Canada. Carr is thrilled to have one of her poems presently orbiting the planet Mars aboard NASA'S MAVEN spacecraft. *www.ferngzcarr.com.*

Lisbon Tawanda Chigwenjere (The Lord's Poet) is a young poet from Harare, Zimbabwe. He was born a twin on the 28th of May 1993. He is currently pursuing an honors degree in Politics and Public Management at the Midlands State University in Gweru, Zimbabwe. Three of his poems, "Days of My Youth", "The Tongue of the Learned", and "Fight, Soldier, Fight", have appeared in *Enter the Gateway*, a Christian poetry anthology published by TL Publishing Group, Florida. His poems have also appeared in Zimbabwean newspapers such as *The Sunday Mail* and *News Day*, and in the official newsletter of the *Midlands State University - The Pulse*. He has been published both in print and media.

Helen Clark is an English Composition Assistant at Rockville High School who also taught English at Montgomery College. She has also worked as a freelance writer and editor, including editing curriculum guides for three television networks. Clark became a Christian and Episcopalian 11 years ago and she is in the second year of Education for Ministry, a four-year course for lay ministers.

Gonzalinho da Costa is the pen name of Joseph I. B. Gonzales, Ph.D. He teaches Methods of Research in Management, and Managerial Statistics at the Ateneo Graduate School of Business, Makati City, Philippines. He is a management research and communication consultant, and Managing Director of Technikos Consulting, Inc. A lover of world literature, he has completed three humanities degrees and writes poetry as a hobby.

Cardiwel Ebuse is a poet of mysticism and the spirit. His influences include writers, like Dante, San Juan de la Cruz, Sor Juana Inés de la Cruz, Góngora, Pascal, and Hopkins.

Dionne Evans is from North Carolina, born and nurtured in this area, the suburbs of Greensboro, NC. After several years of working in the Banking Industry and while working fulltime in an administrative position, she returned to school and graduated from Brookstone College of Business, Greensboro, North Carolina. Evans has always had the desire to write, whether it is poetry, or songs for enjoyment. This is indeed a beautiful gift and she wishes to share it with others.

Charis Froelich is a student attending the University of Windsor for Social Work.

Rick Hartwell is a retired middle school teacher (remember the hormonally-challenged?) living in Southern California. He believes in the succinct, that the small becomes large; and, like the Transcendentalists and William Blake, that the instant contains eternity. Given his "druthers," if he's not writing, Rick would rather still be tailing plywood in a mill in Oregon. He can be reached at *rdhartwell@gmail.com*.

John Kaniecki's work has been published by *Struggle Magazine*, *The Blue Collar Review*, *Burning Books*, *Jerry Jazz*, *IWW Newspaper*, *Protest Poems*, *Flute*, *Black Magnolia*, *Left Curve*, *She Mom*, *Whisper*, *Vox Poetica* and others. He has a chapbook of poetry published on *Cavalcade of Stars*. In addition, his poetry book entitled *Murmurings of a Mad Man* was published last year. Kaniecki's stories have appeared in *Struggle Magazine* and *Cavalcade of Stars*. Additionally, his story "The Sin of A.D.A.M." was published by Witty Bard. He also has an upcoming book of science fiction stories to be published by Witty Bard. Kaniecki's chapbook *The Second Coming of Victoria* was a quarter finalist in the Mary Ballard chapbook contest in 2014. He has been married over nine years to his wife Sylvia. He is a member of the Church of Christ at Chancellor Avenue where he sometimes preaches and works on outreach. Kaniecki worked last as a customer service agent. He is a firm believer in the power of poetry to transform society for the better. The artist he most admires is Woodie Guthrie because he lived what he wrote and what he wrote was wonderful. Kaniecki also recently won the Joe Hill Poetry Labor Prize where he read his poem "Tea With Joe Hill", in front of a crowd of over six hundred people in Banning Park, Los Angeles. He currently serves as secretary for Rhyming Poets International and he is a member of the Revolutionary Poet's Brigade.

James Kelly is a Christian poet living in Northern California; Mr. Kelly has been a journalist for Gannet, and a Travel Book Editor, and worked for the Forest Service in environmental planning in the Pacific Northwest and Alaska. Now, retired Mr. Kelly writes poetry by the Sacramento River and is working on a novel.

Part Texan, part Okie - **Blake Kilgore** fell for a Jersey girl and followed her east. A history teacher by day, he also coaches basketball and performs original folk music. He is grateful for his wife and four sons. Blake's writing has recently appeared or is forthcoming in *The Alembic, Forge, The Bookends Review*, and *ginosko*.

Philip C. Kolin has published seven collections of poems, most recently *Reading God's Handwriting* (Kaufmann Publishing, 2012); *In the Custody of Words* (Franciscan Univ. Press, 2013), and *Departures: A Collection of Poems* (just last month with Negative Capability Press). His poems have appeared in *Christianity and Literature, Spiritus, The Windhover, The Cresset, America, Anglican Theological Review, The Other Journal, Michigan Quarterly Review*, etc.

Jordan Legg is originally from Oshawa, Ontario, and he just received a degree in English and Creative Writing from the University of Windsor. Legg has been published in *Nebula Rift September 2012, Swept Media, Circa Journal 1.2, Strong Verse*, and *Allegory eZine January 2014*. When he's not writing he enjoys drawing, soccer, reading, cycling, and maintaining his beard. Follow him on Twitter at *@JordanLegg2*.

Courtney Liddell is a recent college graduate with a degree in English and a minor in journalism from Shorter University. Reading and writing are passions that define who she is and were formed because of one person, her mother, Cassandra Gail Holland. She started writing poetry after her mother's death in 1998 as a way to cope and grieve, but now poetry is one of her passions.

Native New Yorker **LindaAnn Loschiavo** is a busy dramatist, journalist, theatre critic, and poet. Her stage plays have been seen in the USA and abroad. Her suspense drama "A Worthie Woman All Hir Live" will be filmed this year. Her poems have popped up in *PIF, Measure, Mused, Chronogram, The Cape Rock, Iron Horse Review, tnr, Italian Americana, Rollick Magazine, Windhover*, etc. She's tried her best to be Google-worthy.

Krista S. Mallo has served as an Instructor of English and Writing at Trinity College of Florida since 2013, Adjunct Instructor of Composition at St. Petersburg College since 2002, and holds a Masters degree in English Education from the University of South Florida. Mallo's poetry has been published previously in *Meta: An Interdisciplinary Journal*. She lives in Florida with her husband and four children, and she has recently started blogging *Crying is the First Sign of Life* on *wordpress.com*.

Christina Mengis lives with her husband Chris Mengis, and her stepson Chris Jr. in Oregon. She loves to read, write fiction, and poetry.

Peter Venable has written both free and metric verse for over fifty years. His work has been published in a number of poetry journals, such as *American Vedantist*, *Vineyards*, *The Christian Communicator* (3 issues and one forthcoming), *Third Wednesday*, *Parody*, *The Merton Seasonal*, and forthcoming in *The Laughing Dog*, and *Windhover - A Journal of Christian Literature*. He works as an almost-retired addiction and mental health counselor, and he is graced with a happy marriage, daughter and son-in-law, and Yeshua.

About the Publisher

TL Publishing Group is an independent publisher of poetry and fiction. *The Effects of Grace* is a poetry anthology published under Gateway Literature, an imprint of TL Publishing Group. Gateway Literature books provide readers with inspirational and uplifting poetry.

To learn more, please visit us on the web:

http://torridliterature.com

http://tlpublishing.org